D1572797

HIGH-TECH

Augmented Reality

Cover: Augmented reality uses computer processing and display technology to combine digital graphics with the real world.

Norwood House Press
P.O. Box 316598
Chicago, Illinois 60631

For information regarding Norwood House Press, please visit our website at:
www.norwoodhousepress.com or call 866-565-2900.

Hardcover ISBN: 978-1-59953-886-0
Paperback ISBN: 978-1-68404-117-6

LIBRARY OF CONGRESS CATALOGING-IN-PUBLICATION DATA

Names: Martin, Brett S., author.
Title: Augmented reality / by Brett S. Martin.
Description: Chicago, Illinois : Norwood House Press, [2017] | Audience: Age
   8-12. | Audience: Grade 4 to 6. | Includes bibliographical references and
   index.
Identifiers: LCCN 2017008602 (print) | LCCN 2017020113 (ebook) | ISBN
   9781684041220 (eBook) | ISBN 9781599538860 (library edition : alk. paper)
Subjects: LCSH: Augmented reality--Juvenile literature.
Classification: LCC QA76.9.A94 (ebook) | LCC QA76.9.A94 M36 2017 (print) |
   DDC 006.8--dc23
LC record available at https://lccn.loc.gov/2017008602

302N—072017
Manufactured in the United States of America in North Mankato, Minnesota.

CONTENTS

Note: Words that are **bolded** in the text are defined in the glossary.

CHAPTER 1

Merging Reality with Fiction

In the summer of 2016, people by the thousands gathered in public parks around the country. Each of them stared down at the smartphone in their hands. They were not making calls or texting friends. They were capturing and battling digital monsters in the widely popular game *Pokémon GO*.

On their phones, the players saw an overhead map of their location. Monsters occasionally appeared in specific spots on the map. They showed up in the same place for all players.

At one park, a player cried out that a rare monster was nearby. The crowd surged to the location. People were desperate to add a powerful monster to their collection. The creature appeared on their screens, and they tapped it with their finger.

Their phones' screens changed from an overhead map to a view through the phone's camera. The monster they had tapped was now visible in the real world on the screen. As the phone moved, so did the monster's position. It looked as though it were really there.

The hit game *Pokémon GO* brought hundreds of popular Pokémon characters into the real world.

Players swiped the screen, attempting to catch the monster. Some celebrated as they successfully caught it. Others were disappointed when it ran away. This scene was repeated thousands of times as *Pokémon GO* swept the nation. The game was a popular example of a technology known as augmented reality (AR).

What Is Augmented Reality?

AR works by placing content produced on a computer alongside something that is real. This may happen on a television, on a smartphone screen, or in a special set of glasses. AR lets users bridge the gap between the real world and the digital world.

A woman wears AR glasses at an exhibition in Italy.

Though AR may seem like a recent development, forms of this technology have actually been around since the late 1960s. Many people have used it or at least seen it without even realizing what it was. An example of AR can be seen on televised football games. The yellow first-down line seen on the field is created by a computer. Neither the players nor the fans in the stadium can see the line. The computer **overlays** the line on televised footage from the game. Only TV viewers can see it. This is one of the most commonly seen instances of AR.

Early Stages

Computer scientist Ivan Sutherland created the first AR technology in 1968. He developed a display called the Sword of Damocles. The name came from the Greek story of Damocles, a king with a sword dangling above his head. Sutherland's system hung down from the ceiling above the user, since it was too heavy to wear. A computer created graphics for the display. Users saw a

DID YOU KNOW?

Ivan Sutherland's work changed the way computers are used. He won the Kyoto Prize in Advanced Technology from the Inamori Foundation in 2012 for his work in computer graphics.

three-dimensional **wireframe** placed in the midst of the real world.

Six years later, in 1974, computer artist Myron Krueger created a laboratory he called Videoplace. The lab used film projectors, video cameras, and special hardware to produce an interactive

AR and Sports Coverage

The first-down line in football is the best-known use of AR in sports broadcasting, but this type of technology now appears elsewhere, too. While watching a golf tournament on television, AR could help a viewer see what the course is like. AR can show how far away the green is. It can show where sand traps, obstacles, and other features are located. It also displays a graphic showing the path the ball took after it was hit.

Other sports also use AR. In the NBA, the three-point arc is highlighted in red if a shot is attempted from beyond the line. In tennis, viewers can see where the ball hit the court to tell if it was in or out of bounds. Baseball offers a computer-generated strike zone that lets viewers see where the pitch is thrown and tracks the ball after it is hit, so they can see where it went.

environment. Krueger built his own computer systems to bring together video and graphic images. This created an augmented reality, even though the term had not yet been used before. Videoplace was the first system to allow users to interact with virtual objects.

The term *augmented reality* was first used in 1990 by Tom Caudell, a researcher for the airplane company Boeing. He coined the term to describe a digital display used by aircraft electricians that combined virtual graphics with an actual physical reality. Workers wore a head-mounted digital display that guided them as they assembled complicated electrical wires in airplanes.

Explosion of Uses

AR was introduced into sports in the 1990s. Broadcasters used it to help television viewers see specific things, such as the first-down line in football and fast-moving pucks in hockey.

In 2012, a new device brought more public awareness to AR technology. Google introduced Google Glass, a pair of glasses that used AR. The glasses included a computer, camera, microphone, and all the sensors needed for AR. A tiny display in front of the right eye showed information, such as walking directions or text messages, to the user.

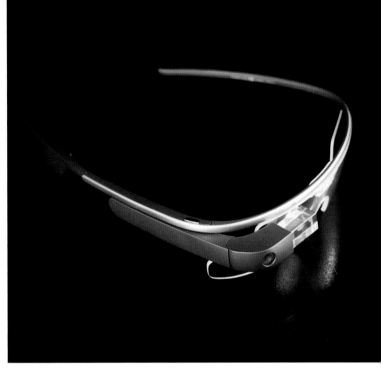

Google Glass was one of the first widespread AR glasses products.

AR reached an even wider audience in the summer of 2016 with the release of *Pokémon GO*. By September of that year, the game had reached 500 million downloads. But AR technology has many uses beyond gaming. Today, AR is used in many industries, including manufacturing. As technology advances, people will continue to find more uses for it.

Making It Possible

The popularity of smartphones over the last several years has contributed to the widespread use of AR. As more people own these phones, more people have easy access to AR. Smartphones include several technologies that make this possible.

At the heart of modern smartphones are powerful computer processors. They are capable of creating complex three-dimensional graphics for AR applications. Phones also contain cameras and large, sharp screens, allowing them to display these graphics alongside the real world. GPS receivers let phones determine their exact locations, making map-based AR possible. Finally, smartphones have sensors called **accelerometers**. These

Today's smartphones are often more powerful than full-sized computers from just a few years ago.

sensors detect when the phone moves. This way, the view of the AR graphics can shift as needed. This maintains the illusion of the objects existing in the real world.

Changing Our View of the World

AR has become so common that many people barely notice it. It is used for

Release 4 screws ⬡ 10.0

A worker demonstrates how AR technology can be used in factories.

getting GPS driving directions. People see it on television in sports broadcasts. They interact with it when using smartphone apps. AR can be used to shop, allowing customers to try on glasses virtually before buying them. Many people now use AR for their work. AR technology can give them instant access to visual information. This helps them be more productive.

Many business executives, analysts, and technology experts expect AR to play a big role in people's lives. As technology improves and people realize its benefits, the use of AR will increase. Tim Cook, the CEO of the computer company Apple,

Making Money with AR

Pokémon GO has shown that AR games can be big business. Combining the popular characters of the Pokémon video game series with AR technology proved extremely popular with players. The game was free to download, but players could spend money on extra items within the game. News reports estimated that the game made $600 million in its first 90 days of release. It was the fastest mobile game ever to reach that mark.

Huge crowds of people could be found playing Pokémon GO around the world.

said using AR will become routine: "I do think that a significant portion of the population of developed countries, and eventually all countries, will have AR experiences every day, almost like eating three meals a day. It will become that much a part of you."

CHAPTER 2

A Technology Boost

Though AR has come a long way in recent years, the field still faces challenges. One of these challenges is the same one many other modern technologies face: large up-front expenses. Businesses may face high costs in designing AR devices, and companies need to get a return on that investment.

A second obstacle is also common to many technologies. It is the inability of the hardware to meet new demands. Early computers and cell phones were not powerful enough to present the vivid graphics that make AR special. Faster processors have solved many of these problems. But even today, companies work to improve hardware to make the AR experience smoother, more useful, and easier to use.

Natural Progression

As computing power increases, so does the progress of AR. The first portable computers were laptops. Today many

Many advanced AR devices were still in the testing phases by 2017. Companies were making rapid progress on incredible new AR systems.

people have smartphones. Even smaller **wearable** technology could be the next step in this process. People could begin wearing AR devices daily. Rather than having to look at a screen, the person would see AR images directly in their vision. Google Glass is one early example of this style of AR.

In addition to technical advances, other specific elements have led to

and realistic blending of the virtual and physical worlds. This makes it easy to see information without being bothered by it looking unrealistic and cartoonish. Experience in developing AR applications has sharpened software developers' skills.

The World of Holograms

A hologram is a three-dimensional image. It is a picture or video that shows an entire object. The viewer can walk around the hologram and see it from all angles. Special glasses are not needed to view a hologram.

Early holograms were invented in 1947. They became more realistic in the 1960s with the invention of lasers, which can be used to record and display the images. Today, holograms can be

wider use of AR applications. The first is having meaningful content available to use. Software developers have to make AR apps that people actually want to try. The second is the convincing

Augmented Reality in the Movies

AR has been used in many well-known movies. One example is *Who Framed Roger Rabbit*, in which actual people and Looney Tunes cartoon characters shared screen time. The 1988 movie featured human actors interacting with Donald Duck, Bugs Bunny, and many others. More recently, the Alvin and the Chipmunks movies have mixed human actors with computer-generated talking animals. Other movies, such as the Iron Man films, take a more realistic approach. The main character, Tony Stark, interacts with AR technology that is far beyond what is available today. He uses hand motions and voice commands to display and manipulate complex holograms that seem to float in space around him.

The Alvin and the Chipmunks films place computer-generated animals in the real world alongside human actors.

projected in vehicles and homes to create an AR experience.

The online retailer Amazon is working on an AR system for the home. The

to try out new furniture or decorations before buying them.

Holograms can play a role in live concerts. At the popular Coachella festival in 2012, concert goers were shocked and thrilled when a realistic hologram of the deceased rap star Tupac Shakur began dancing to a song. Other celebrities who have "performed" as holograms after their deaths include Michael Jackson and Elvis Presley.

The Future of Driving

Getting directions through phones and GPS devices is nothing new. The first GPS system for consumer use came out in 1989, and GPS systems have been built into cars for several years. Until now, these driving directions have usually

company says, "The augmented reality may range in sophistication from partial augmentation, such as projecting a single image onto a surface and monitoring user interaction with the image, to full augmentation where an entire room is transformed into another reality for the user's senses." Customers could use AR

AR systems can display basic information to a driver on the windshield.

been displayed on small screens. Now, with the help of AR, directions can show up on your windshield. Drivers won't have to look away from the road to see driving directions. Several companies are already using early forms of this kind of technology. For example, Jaguar Land Rover uses laser holograms to project information, such as speed and direction, onto the windshield.

Other Digital Realities

AR is not the only technology that brings together the physical and digital worlds. Virtual reality is also gaining in popularity. It brings users into interactive, **immersive** worlds that are entirely computer generated. To experience these worlds, users must wear special goggles or headsets. Extended reality involves people-controlled devices, such as drones. These devices move through spaces that are apart from the people controlling them.

Virtual reality headsets block out the real world from the user's vision.

Health Risks

The downsides to AR are the potential health and safety risks. AR glasses can block part of your vision. Holograms or other images may hinder your ability to see straight in front of you. Information off to the side can impede your peripheral vision. Having your vision even partially blocked can throw off your sense of balance. Anything that obstructs your vision can cause you to misjudge how fast you are moving and cause motion sickness. AR in your vehicle could cause you to midjudge the speed of oncoming cars. This may slow down your reaction time, which could cause an accident.

People engaged in AR can end up too focused on their smartphones and ignore the reality around them. Several *Pokémon GO* players were hurt while concentrating on the game. One man crashed his car into a tree, and a teenager was hit by a car when crossing a busy highway while playing.

Both AR developers and users play a role in minimizing these risks. Developers can work to create AR systems that minimize distractions and avoid blocking vision as much as possible. Users operate

DID YOU KNOW?

Digital learning simulations using AR can help educate students. Simulations increase the amount of information students remember and make students more engaged. In one study, students who participated in digital learning simulations had a 23 percent higher achievement rating than those who did not.

AR applications responsibly by making sure to pay attention to the real world around them.

CHAPTER 3

Working and Playing

AR has the potential to improve workers' efficiency. This effect can be seen in airplane construction, the field where the term *augmented reality* originated. Boeing factory trainees assembling a mock airplane wing were 30 percent faster and 90 percent more accurate using AR instructions on tablets than trainees using traditional written instructions.

Likewise, warehouse workers who wore AR glasses made fewer errors and were 25 percent more efficient. The smart glasses guided workers through their job of picking the correct items to fulfill orders. Improving **logistics** in this way is important for companies. Giving more information to workers helps them save time while working. This saves the company money, making it more competitive.

A steel company found similar results. AR helmets guided workers through each step in a procedure. A camera in the helmet identified when a task was finished, and then it gave the next instruction. As a

SERVICE & MAINTENANCE AUGMENTED REALITY

Technician

AR technology has many potential uses for industrial workers.

result, worker productivity increased 40 percent. There was a 50 percent reduction in factory downtime, or periods in which employees were not working. Because of these types of results, some companies are using AR more often.

Some people worried about being secretly filmed by Google Glass users.

Google Glass

Google Glass was introduced in 2012. It was the first pair of wearable AR glasses for consumers. The product quickly became famous in pop culture. It was named one of *Time* magazine's "Best Inventions of the Year." The animated show *The Simpsons* had an episode with the character Homer wearing them.

Well-known celebrities including Oprah, Beyoncé, Jennifer Lawrence, and Prince Charles wore them. Even models wore them in fashion shows.

Google Glass let users connect to the Internet, ask Google Maps for directions, and give voice commands to do tasks such as take a picture. Unlike other virtual or AR gear that is big, boxy, or bulky, Google Glass looks sleek and similar to reading glasses.

However, public opinion soon turned against the product. People who wore it criticized its short battery life, high price,

Google Glass Explorers

Google Glass was never widely released to the general public. In 2013, Google began selling pairs of the glasses to people it called "Google Glass Explorers." These people paid $1,500 each to try out the new technology. Google's promotional videos for the product showed people skydiving, getting directions, and dictating text messages. But in the real world, many users found that the glasses were not as useful as they had hoped.

and problems when using it. The glasses also raised concerns over privacy. People worried that someone wearing Google Glass could record them in secret and then embarrass them by posting the video on social media. Movie theaters banned them over fears users would record films. Other places, including casinos and restaurants, also banned them to protect customers' privacy. One technology reviewer called Google Glass "the worst product of all time." Google stopped offering the glasses in 2015. Although they are no longer available, Google Glass opened the door for later AR products.

Microsoft HoloLens

Microsoft HoloLens is the first self-contained, holographic computer that lets users engage with digital content and interact with holograms. One reviewer called it "the first augmented-reality

A Microsoft stage presentation demonstrated how users could play *Minecraft* with HoloLens.

device done right." The technology runs completely on its own. Users do not need to connect it to a smartphone, tablet, or personal computer.

The product is a headset that looks like a cross between goggles and a visor. Users look through lenses to see computer-generated objects. Unlike with virtual reality headsets, users can also see the real world around them.

The lenses and projectors display holograms in a small space in the center of your view. If the hologram is a person, the user can only see part of that person, such as the head and shoulders. If the user looks down at his or her feet, he or she will not see the face. If the user looks to either side, the hologram disappears.

Meta 2

The Meta 2 is another AR headset system. It projects holograms onto glasses. Users can interact with these holograms using their hands. The holograms are treated like physical objects, so users can pick them up, move them, or turn them over for a different view. Meta 2 uses sensors to track the user's position and detect his or her hand movements. It creates a model of the world around the user in **real time**. The virtual hologram objects will stay where they are placed until the user moves them again.

One drawback to Meta 2 is that it must be connected to a computer with a cable. This restricts where users can go and what they can see while wearing it. However, the upside is that this system offers high-quality graphics.

The predecessor to Meta 2, Meta 1, was developed with funding from the popular **crowdfunding** website Kickstarter.

A user tries on the Meta 1 headset.

Using the site, the makers raised $194,444 from 501 people. They promised that the system would "finally deliver a natural interface between the virtual world and reality."

Magic Leap

The Magic Leap headset generated a lot of buzz before it was even released. "We are building a new kind of contextual computer," said founder and CEO Rony Abovitz. "We're doing something really, really different."

The difference with Magic Leap is in the optics. The headset tricks the eye into focusing far away, even though the screen is just a few inches away. This feels more natural to the eye and allows visuals to appear more realistic. The company is keeping the design of this technology secret.

Magic Leap lets users place information around a room, such as weather forecasts, charts, and online shopping websites. Instead of having to read this kind of information through a phone or computer screen, a person can walk around the room and interact with the holograms.

Snapchat has become one of the hottest social media apps among teenagers.

Snapchat

AR technology is used for fun, too. Snapchat is a popular social media app for smartphones that lets people share photos and videos. Users can communicate with friends by sending pictures. Snapchat has become wildly popular among teens and young adults. Most people in that age group carry cell phones and use them frequently. They like that Snapchat offers a fast, effective, and fun way to communicate. The app is also one of today's most common uses of AR.

Snapchat uses filters that place masks, designs, and other graphics on images of people's faces. Facial recognition software applies different effects, such

DID YOU KNOW?

Snapchat images are seen by 41 percent of all 18- to 34-year-olds in the United States on any given day. The app has 150 million users and 10 billion video views each day.

in videos. The stickers stay in place, no matter where the camera moves. For example, users can stick a smiling face emoji on a dog as it walks around the house. One technology analyst said, "We think that Snapchat is evolving beyond just 'another social media platform' and could be headed to be the first 'social augmented reality platform.'"

Pokémon GO

Pokémon GO put AR on the map for a new generation. Unlike video games that keep people sitting in front of their televisions or computers, this one got users out of the house. The idea was to capture Pokémon in real-life yards, neighborhoods, public landmarks, or anywhere else they might be wandering.

as a surprised or scared look. Users can give human faces a pair of cat ears and whiskers, clown makeup, a waterfall gushing out of the mouth, or a range of other digital additions.

Snapchat also has three-dimensional stickers that users can place on objects

A Revolution in Gaming

Pokémon GO is based on the long-running series of Pokémon video games. The AR game broke new ground for mobile games. In less than a week, it became the most downloaded app in Apple's App Store. Users spent an average of 43 minutes playing each day, which is more time than was spent on Snapchat and Facebook. As *New Yorker* writer Om Malik put it, "To say it has spread like wildfire is to exaggerate the power of wildfires."

Pokémon GO users show off the game's overhead AR map view.

The free mobile phone app uses location tracking, cameras, and three-dimensional graphics to place the animated monsters in users' actual surroundings. Gamers can train their Pokémon or get supplies in real-world locations. The game is an example of a social AR experience. It encourages people to play together. Gamers can join with friends to search for Pokémon and battle gamers from other teams.

CHAPTER 4

High-Tech Solutions

The future of AR is bright. It can make information available faster and more easily, no matter where the user is. This technology is poised to change how people access information, just as search engines and smartphones have done in the past. As devices and software improve, AR will find its way into many careers and parts of everyday life. Companies are expected to continue offering new apps and content. This would enable new abilities.

Getting the Bad Guys

AR could soon be added to police forces. The technology can help officers with investigations. The Dutch national police is one police force planning to use it. Officers will have shoulder-mounted cameras and smartphones attached to their wrists. This way, they can take pictures and make digital notes at crime scenes. AR technology will allow them to share those notes with other officers at the scene.

Wearing tiny cameras mounted on glasses or clothing will help make AR technology more accessible to police officers.

When the case ends up in a courtroom, AR can present critical information to the jury. This makes it easier for juries to see evidence and for lawyers to place evidence over pictures of the actual crime scene to show how events took place. "The advantage of augmented reality is the potential ability to recreate a crime scene for a jury," says a professor of criminal justice.

The technology can also help pick a suspect out of a crowd. By using AR to pin a special icon on a suspect, the police can follow the person wherever he or she goes. That way, if someone commits a crime and then runs into a mall full of people, the AR technology can keep track of him or her.

Other emergency responders, such as firefighters and paramedics, can also benefit from AR. When they arrive at a fire, crime scene, or accident, the situation can be chaotic. Headgear with AR technology can show them where to

AR glasses can put information in view while leaving a person's hands free to do other important tasks.

go. They can also see where gas or water lines are located underground so they can be shut off.

A New Shopping Experience

AR has become part of today's shopping experience. According to a survey, nearly two-thirds of adults in the United States said AR has influenced where they shop. "AR is reshaping the way shoppers experience and engage with retailers," one analyst noted. "We are seeing even the most traditional brands start to include this experiential element in stores, largely driven by customer interest."

AR can bring a picture, product label, or shop display to life. People can see items, such as a sweatshirt, in different colors and with product information. Shoppers can learn more about the product, such as the material it is made from and where it is made.

DID YOU KNOW?

A survey showed that three-quarters of shoppers were interested in using AR to see product differences, such as other colors or styles. Approximately 65 percent wanted to use it to learn more about products.

Shoppers can use AR to quickly test different variations of products.

AR can provide virtual stores that do not have to be physically built. This saves companies the big expense of having to buy real estate, build a store, and hire employees. Instead, customers can use phones or computers to browse virtual aisles, tap or click on the screen to learn more about products, and add items to their shopping carts.

Shoppers enjoy AR because it is personal and interactive. Unlike other online shopping, in which people have to imagine how a product will look in real life, AR removes the guesswork. Users can use a smartphone and an app to see how they will look in a new shirt, for example, or how a new lamp will look in a living room.

From Car Owner to Mechanic

At one time, many people fixed their own vehicles. That changed as cars became more complex. With AR, it is changing back. As one technology website declared, "Anyone can be a mechanic." One app virtually labels engine parts. It gives

Reshaping Retail

A study called "The Impact of Augmented Reality on Retail" found out just how much AR technology influences shoppers. Six out of ten shoppers prefer stores that offer AR, and 75 percent purchased items they did not originally plan on buying because of it. In addition, more than half of people said they would spend more time in a store if they could use AR. About 40 percent of shoppers say they would pay more for a product if they could use AR to try it out before buying it.

animated demonstrations on how to carry out minor repairs. This helps car owners save money by performing maintenance and making fixes themselves.

At least one car manufacturer, Hyundai, offers an AR owner's manual app that lets users access information, including how-to videos and three-dimensional images, from a smartphone or tablet.

Digital graphics represent different parts of the engine and interior. When a user taps on a graphic, it offers step-by-step instructions for tasks ranging from changing the air filter to connecting a phone to the car.

Professional mechanics can also benefit from AR. AR technology wirelessly connects to a vehicle to determine the

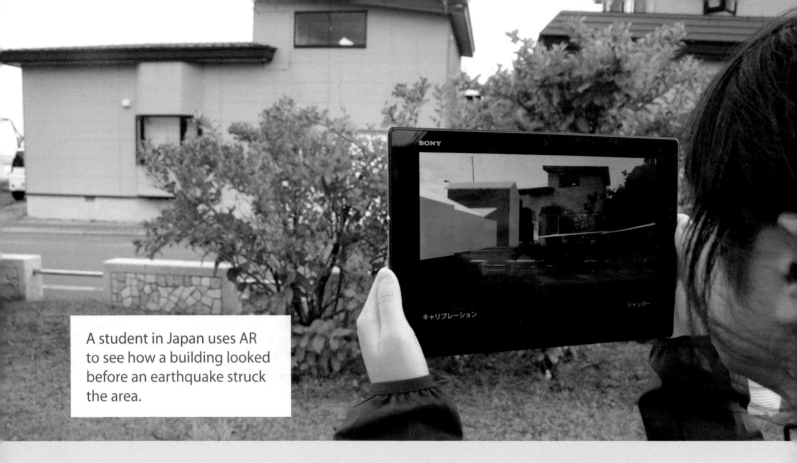

A student in Japan uses AR to see how a building looked before an earthquake struck the area.

status of the vehicle's systems. An app then walks the mechanic through tests to identify a problem as well as the tools and parts needed to make the repair.

Interactive Teaching

Learning no longer has to be confined to textbooks and teacher demonstrations. AR offers new ways for students to

Augmented Reality Sandbox

The University of California, Davis, combined a small box of sand with AR to let users create mountains, lakes, and rivers right before their eyes. With just a few swipes of the hand, a user can simulate a tsunami, create a landslide, or make a volcano erupt. The AR sandbox is a teaching tool for the college's Department of Geography. "We work with a lot of topographic maps, and you are looking at a flat piece of paper. A lot of the times it's hard to grasp that concept," said Greg Beringer, a graduate student who built the sandbox. The sandbox lets students see maps in three dimensions to gain a better understanding.

AR sandboxes are now in use at multiple museums around the world. Users of all ages can try them.

learn. Teachers can add digital graphics to materials, such as books, maps, or anatomy charts. This emphasizes specific content for a lesson.

An article in the *Chronicle of Higher Education* notes, "Video and computer games are commonly criticized for isolating players from reality, but augmented-reality developers who work in higher education see the technology as a way to accomplish just the opposite." Instead of merely explaining the force of gravity that causes a ball to roll down a hill, teachers can use AR to show a ball rolling and add graphics that represent gravity.

Students who learn with AR seem more focused on their lessons. The technology can help students of all ages. For example, three-dimensional blocks can help young students learn basic math. High school students learning about ancient Egypt can see how artifacts were used. There are now more than 200 AR apps available for the classroom.

DID YOU KNOW?

By the year 2020, industry forecasters estimated the market for AR will reach $100 billion. They also estimated 21 million pairs of smart glasses would be shipped to retailers for consumers to buy in that year.

Helping with Building and Construction

Designers, architects, and contractors can use AR to see how parts and systems fit together in a building or remodeling project. This can make the construction process faster, easier, and less likely to include mistakes. Proposed plans can be placed over existing blueprints to see how additions or changes will blend with current structures. This gives workers a better understanding of exactly where plumbing pipes, electrical cables, and heating vents will be located, as well as how those systems overlap.

Seeing projects at various stages of the building process also helps contractors identify potential problems. They can

AR tools can let construction workers quickly and easily measure the parts of a structure.

virtually walk through the building to make sure the construction meets building codes and check that items such as light switches are in convenient locations.

Construction projects are often plagued by problems. Because contractors use printed blueprints, making changes, sharing information, and visualizing the finished project can be hard. Using AR more often in the $10 trillion global construction industry can help projects stay on budget and on schedule.

AR can help on the inside of buildings, too. It lets interior designers and building owners make informed choices on decorations, furniture, and layouts. For instance, they can see what furniture will look like in a home or office before buying it. This ensures the furniture will fit with the building's design, space, and colors.

Shaping Health Care

Experts suggest that AR is set to change health care, too. AR can help with a variety of needs, such as training medical students, assisting with surgeries, and helping patients who suffer from an illness. AR medical apps show the human body and how it works. For instance, an app can place digital information onto a picture of a human skeleton to teach students.

One product, called Eyes-On Glass, is a wearable technology that helps doctors and nurses find veins when giving shots or administering intravenous fluids. The head-mounted device uses light, ultrasound, and other technology to locate the patient's blood vessels through the skin. This reduces the time and pain involved with inserting needles.

Patients can also benefit. AR lets patients scan drug labels to learn how to take medicine correctly and find out about possible side effects. Guidelines may be easier to understand through AR on a mobile device than from a printed description.

What's Next

There is a huge market for AR. More than 100 million people already use it. Many people working in technology expect AR to become even more commonplace. AR technology is improving rapidly, and it appears the field will continue to grow, find new uses, and be accepted as part of everyday life.

accelerometers (ak-sel-uh-ROM-i-terz): Instruments for measuring movement.

crowdfunding (KROWD-fun-ding): A way of raising money online from a large group of people.

immersive (ih-MUR-siv): Surrounding a user and feeling realistic.

logistics (loh-JIS-tiks): The planning, implementation, and coordination of details of operations in a business.

overlays (oh-ver-LEYZ): places something, such as a graphic, over something else.

real time (REEL tyme): Having changes that take place immediately, as people experience them.

wearable (WAIR-uh-buhl): Able to be incorporated into an accessory or item of clothing worn on the body.

wireframe (WY-re fraym): An image of a three-dimensional object made up of interconnected lines that form a skeletal outline of the object.

FOR MORE INFORMATION

Books

Brett S. Martin, *Virtual Reality*. Chicago, IL: Norwood House Press, 2018. Virtual reality shares much in common with augmented reality. The book provides more information about this related technology.

Marne Ventura, *Google Glass and Robotics Innovator Sebastian Thrun*. Minneapolis, MN: Lerner Publications, 2014. Sebastian Thrun worked on Google Glass and many other cool technology projects. The book shows how he developed these technologies and helped change the course of AR history.

Therese Naber, *How the Computer Changed History*. Minneapolis, MN: Abdo Publishing, 2016. Augmented reality is made possible by computers that are smaller and more powerful than ever before. The book explains how computers went from machines the size of whole rooms to tiny devices that fit inside a pair of glasses.

Websites

The Atlantic: Imagination in the Augmented-Reality Age (https://www.theatlantic.com/education/archive/2016/08/play-in-the-augmented-reality-age/494597/) This article includes more information about the *Pokémon GO* phenomenon and what it may mean for the future of games.

The Guardian: Augmented Reality (https://www.theguardian.com/technology/2010/mar/21/augmented-reality-iphone-advertising) This article discusses how AR technology may change many parts of our everyday lives.

INDEX

Brett S. Martin has more than 20 years of writing experience. He has worked as a reporter, editor, director of public relations, and president of his own media company. He has written for more than two dozen magazines and has written several fiction and nonfiction books. He has also volunteered as a youth football coach for nine seasons. Martin lives in Shakopee, Minnesota, with his wife and two teenage sons.